The Tree Poets

Flames of Ice

Kay Channon

Kate Garrett

Elizabeth Gibson

First published 2025 by The Hedgehog Poetry Press

Published in the UK by
The Hedgehog Poetry Press
5, Coppack House
Churchill Avenue
Clevedon
BS21 6QW

www.hedgehogpress.co.uk

ISBN: 978-1-913499-87-7

Copyright © Mark Davidson 2025

The right of Mark Davidson to be identified as the editor of this work has been asserted in accordance with the Copyright, Designs and Patents Act 1988. All rights for individual works retained by the respective author.

All rights reserved. No part of this publication may be reproduced, stored in or introduced into a retrieval system, or transmitted in any form, or by any means (electronic, mechanical, photocopying, recording or otherwise) without prior written permissions of the publisher. Any person who does any unauthorised act in relation to this publication may be liable for criminal prosecution and civil claims for damages,

9 8 7 6 5 4 3 2 1

A CIP Catalogue record for this book is available from the British Library.

Kay Channon 7

    Paper Boats 9
    Thundercloud 10
    Window Pane 11
    Mundane Ghosts 12
    Forbidden Fruit 13

Kate Garrett 15

    Cinders 17
    Effigy 18
    These wings will not carry you over an ocean 19
    Grandpa's going hunting 20
    Flammability limits 21

Elizabeth Gibson 23

    A cave 24
    The chocolatier 25
    Perpignan sestina 26
    Peaches 28
    Sant-Vicens 29

KAY CHANNON

PAPER BOATS

Walking the shattered crystal lines of my father's face
I make paper boats to cross the river
revising the ripest ripples
in the wake of lost memories

The droplets dance in the needy whirlpool
wanting to cling to the clear reflection at the edge of my fingertips
bright colours stain the water without words
I've forgotten how to forget his name
I've forgotten the shoes he wore

There has been too much death
too much silence

The invisible captains steer boldly through fragile confusion, wonder, and grief
Has he replaced my blood with comfortable emptiness?
Or adopted another to erase the pain?

The sails, twitching, convey an impossible semaphore
another language
we stand at either side of the river's edge, helpless...

THUNDERCLOUD

Falling through my thundercloud
Weightless for this wakeful day
So close to night,
Rocksteady.

Drowning in deceitful rain
A dryness rich like sandpaper
Scratching, tearing, grinding away
Through and through to the bone.

I set aside my dreams
For the turning world and its whispers
The circle encircles the fire without flame
Tears yet to fall crystallise my brain
And freeze. Breathe.

Pain nor joy hides its face for you
They stand a reminder of humanity
In space instilled with willingness
Magnetised by conflict...

Will you speak?
Will you speak to my hesitation?
I will never ask you to save me
Will you speak?

Delayed decay in a loveless way
For the heart is strong but out of time
And words on beauty's paper bleed
As that which is written does not concede anything
Let alone what it means to be

Thunder cracks, crashes and moans
A never-ending chorus in the name of noise
I listen speechless in the wake of its echo,
I will never ask you to save me...

WINDOW PANE

Shifting through the obscured window pane
your white eye glistens

With knowledge sighing in my soul
I blink away the tears of tortured time at the ending of tomorrow

The paper planes we made lay screwed up in the waste paper basket
along with the wishes that once brought them to life
their pointed shells a bitter unwanted muse

The stranger in the glass is not recognised
silent and still
as the clouds fall and dress up the future in scattered pain
for the dread of the day

MUNDANE GHOSTS

A place of natural relief
you can see both sides
hear everything

Chocolates replaced with bad tasting smarties
bleeps measuring heartbeats

A God passes by with a face you can't quite place –
maybe he's been here before?

I wonder how many have slept in these sheets
attached to a line like mine

With a flinch
shorter than a blink
I enter a state of remembrance
barely noticing the mundane ghost
walking across the floor...

FORBIDDEN FRUIT

I've bitten off certain death
its hollowness gapes in blackness without an edge
a thankless cage against a helpless backdrop

The silence catches me, deafening,
scratching at my throat like disintegrating charcoal

I ask again for a map of my destination
only to be met by emptiness
widening in a narrow hole

KATE GARRETT

CINDERS

The one thing he taught her
is that most things end up crumbled
in the grate. She watched his mam
throw an old pair of trainers in once:
rubber smoke covered the room,
oily and black. But still they burned
and burned until only the soles
remained – misshapen, changed,
lumps of them cooling outside
in the ash pan the next morning.

EFFIGY

Smoke-cocooned in the sacral
end of the year
outside the back door
swaying in time
to the ale in my glass
I loop my cigarette
in the path of fire-blossoms
unfurling across
the almost-winter sky.

Friends have drifted
home to sleep
and dream of revolutions.

Alone in the rain-smouldered night
ancestral memories awaken
this unfamiliar stirring in my stomach—
like devotion branded treason
like gunpowder waiting to flash-bang-devour
like an uprising I am not leading.

I can't see the stars.
He doesn't believe in ghosts or me.
I bide my time.

THESE WINGS WILL NOT CARRY YOU OVER AN OCEAN

Manduca sexta (tobacco hawk moth)

Little lanterns shine just beyond our bonfire
where I sit listening for the snap of wood
becoming ash – exchanging a long Saturday
of heat for blue-black relief around the flames.

Creatures in the trees scout for light, swoop
towards any hint of it, wingspan wider
than my dimpled outstretched hands,
waves of hair waiting for six lithe legs to find me –

then the landing: heavy-bodied, flapping and gone,
simply insects chasing the night – but my memory
of golden stripes, a feathered
bullet, steals my August sleep.

Castillege mi (mother Shipton moth)

She tells you some years later, on a whisk
of wings, how prophecies stay hidden
because no one is paying attention:
cloaks and crooked legs and caves –
none of these are secrets.

The outline of her face in flight
seeking auras cast by outstretched
arms of galaxies – second sight
is not a gift for sun-soaked butterflies.

GRANDPA'S GOING HUNTING

Even at my smallest I would not fit
in such a tiny hide, but he
sang his version of the song
to me and meant every word:

*bye baby bunting / papaw's going hunting / I'm off
to catch a rabbit skin / to wrap our little Katey in*

– a spindly pine child barely taller
than meadow grass, given fresh
fluffed squirrels' tails for luck.
I would pull the fur through the space

between my fingers, examine blood-
sealed stub, imagining a life in the branches
of trees while grandma fried the meat
for our supper. My mother branded it cruelty,

but he wanted me to see the sum of a life
and death on earth wasn't bought in the store.
If grandpa came back with an empty
truck during deer season, we felt the defeat –

he'd never hunt for sport, nor for survival
anymore, but a sewn-in instinct
to be more than just a hand flipping
pages on a calendar. The kill

was born of the same force guiding
the growth in his garden: the gift
of tomatoes, green beans, jars lining
our basement shelves each winter.

FLAMMABILITY LIMITS

Close July – more a creature than a month –
chased me indoors, or under the water, where
I'd be secure against the blast of county fair tractor
pulls, cherry bombs, sunburn on lakeshore sand.

I'd float up to my chin in the murk, bluegills
stalking my ankles, the sun dropping
low into the monster's mouth.

These days when a golden anger
torches gentle English mornings

I daydream specks of old summer
beneath maple trees, the gravel tracks
seething in the heat, skin cooled inside out

by salted watermelon. I conjure timewasting
and grass-itch legs. Near nightfall I am primed
to nail a string of M80s to the post – spark the fuse,
stand close, and swallow each popgun explosion.

ELIZABETH GIBSON

A CAVE

How do I explain my love?

I cannot, except to tell you that there is a cave somewhere
in a cliff far from anywhere, and the sea washes herself
against it, sometimes viciously, sometimes tenderly,
but she never stops and the cave knows nobody will ever
visit it and see what it may hide, what rubies or shells,
that centuries will pass and it will go undiscovered

and it doesn't care

because it has the sea, and if it weren't for the sea it
wouldn't be at all; she made it, without realising there was
another hole in the earth because of her, that got deeper
and taller and more elegant because she washed against
it, sometimes viciously, sometimes tenderly, and that
all the cave needed to achieve contentment in its existence

was to know she would never stop.

First published in 'Far Off Places'

THE CHOCOLATIER

How has nobody eaten you yet? I would coat you in sugar, cut you the prettiest paper nest in which to curl, even tie a golden ribbon around your neck. I would surround you with cinnamon and ginger,

cardamom and mint. I would craft you, make fudge of your hair and caramel of your eyes. Or maybe you are better out in the wide world, facing seas of salt and trying not to lose your sweetness.

PERPIGNAN SESTINA

In the shadow of Mount Canigou she dreams blood,
tears and a small soft form, someone who will remain
without question. On the dusky Canet shore she waits
in a merciful daze while the sea laps, so shiny like oil,
and the sky is purple – really, like a painting by Dalí,
as she wakes reluctantly in the centre of the universe.

She cups the soft air, cradling, caressing the universe.
The sun-ice on the Canigou sparkles like fresh blood
or her school artwork, silver swans after those Dalí
made elephants. She never thought she would remain
the only swan, with feathers clogged useless with oil
and no low belly of calf. She knows the elephant waits

by its relative's grave; she has no relative so she waits
by the sea, scales the mountains, consoles the universe
for fish limp in nets or snails under feet. She tries to oil
the aching cogs of that great machine of salt and blood
that declares she will be granted no kin but will remain
alone in terrains of gold and flame and drought by Dalí.

As a high-strung twelve-year-old she specialised in Dalí,
would explain the secret of that sleepy being that waits
peacefully in another realm, how the long lashes remain
still, yet to be dragged by slack clocks into the universe.
The other kids looked nonplussed as she felt her blood
pounding with passion, tears mixing thick with the oil

in the painting and as she sat down, simmering like oil
when the flame hits, she knew she would seek out Dalí
in his centre of the universe, his city of heat and blood
and garnets, the line of peaks where the Canigou waits,
the sea at Canet, kind, cold and near, and the universe
that scoops you up in its arms and swears it will remain

by you until you have to stand and leave it, will remain
by you whenever you hurt or want. A sky painted in oil,
indigo and violet: it is there, she is it, she is the universe,
she is painted and she is the painter. She is just like Dalí;
she should etch out her fate, she must, and so she waits
for the day she will make it rain on the hot land. Blood,

blood will spill over her hands as she sobs her joy, blood
will make her an elephant, will wake the child that waits
asleep, a face in the ether, drifting, in a painting by Dalí.

First published in 'Cake' and won Second Prize in the Manchester Global Health Poetry Competition 2018

PEACHES

We'd left Carcassonne, left peering at
diamond skies through tiny holes in
ancient walls
and draped our tired selves across the
too-soft seats of a coach bound
for Montpellier.

The weather was fractious as ever; our
eyes itched. And then, in a breath,
there they were:
weird, stubbly little things, pulsing
pink-white blossom, like something
from the moon.

Rain drifted in and the peach trees
pricked the greyness: fairy lights,
gulping sheets of salt.
Like when I see a tree bloom in the
middle of the night. It never does
fail to surprise me.

First published in 'The Cluny'

SANT-VICENS

On a ground burnt raw with lizards
watch the marching caterpillars.
Perfect lines, observe the pilgrims
in the days of sun and lemons.

Grazing from a raspberry punnet,
dodge the glaze-eyed octopuses.
Pigeons prompt a storm of blossoms
in the days of sun and lemons.

Capybaras swim, they told you,
in the lake that hugs the bamboo.
Never do they cross your vision
in the days of sun and lemons.

Golden tiles display their lustre,
hexagons like sheets of sugar.
Silence hums like bees and dragons
in the days of sun and lemons.

Watch the rabbits leap by sunset,
night curl round the palms that forget
that the world will wake and go on
after days of sun and lemons.